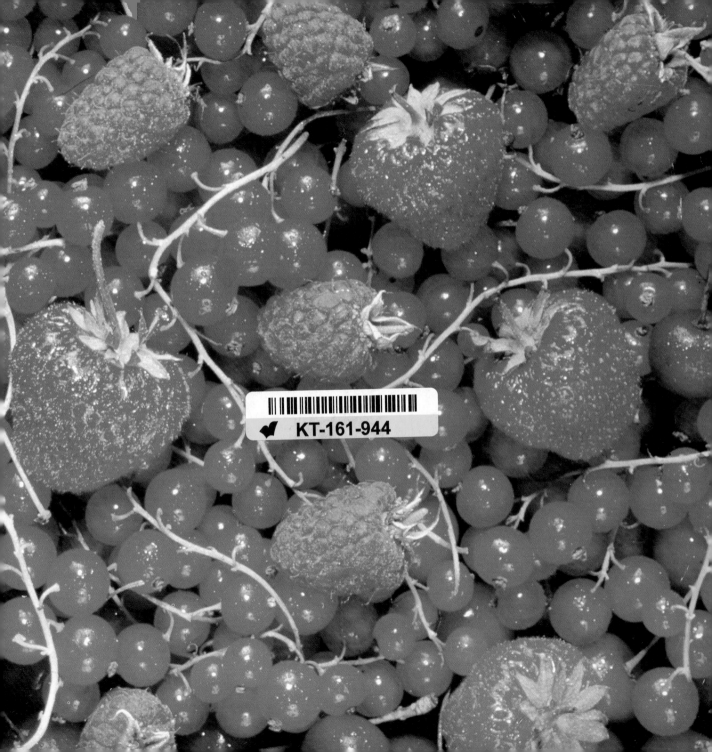

A Dorling Kindersley Book

Text Christopher Maynard
Project Editor Jane Donnelly
Art Editor Melanie Whittington
Deputy Managing Art Editor Jane Horne
Deputy Managing Editor Mary Ling
Production Ruth Cobb
Consultant Theresa Greenaway
Picture Researcher Tom Worsley

Additional photography by David Murray, Stephen Shott, David
Johnson, Peter Chadwick, Dave King, Stephen Oliver, Ian O'Leary,
Tim Ridley, Geoff Dann, Andy Crawford, Philip Dowell,
Peter Anderson, Jane Burton, Mike Dunning

First published in Great Britain in 1997
by Dorling Kindersley Limited,
9 Henrietta Street, London WC2E 8PS
Visit us on the World Wide Web at http://www.dk.com

Reprinted 1997

Copyright © 1997 Dorling Kindersley Limited, London

A CIP catalogue record for this book is available
from the British Library.

ISBN: 0-7513-5514-3

Colour reproduction by Chromagraphics, Singapore
Printed and bound in Italy by L.E.G.O.

The publisher would like to thank the following for their kind
permission to reproduce their photographs:

t top, b bottom, l left, r right, c centre, BC back cover, FC front cover

The Anthony Blake Photo Library: 7cr, 7crb, 5cb, 6tl;
Cephas Picture Library: 7cl; Tony Stone Images: Paul Chesley BC c,
10-11c, Peter Correz 18-19c, Nick Gunderson 21br, David Olsen
16-17c, FC, Joel Papavoine endpapers, Christel Rosenfeld 8-9c, Andy
Sacks 12-13c, 15br, Don Smetzer 14-15c, Joe Solem FC c, Denis
Waugh 11br, Zane Williams 16bl; Zefa Pictures: 6bl

Contents

WHY

are pineapples prickly?

Questions children ask about food

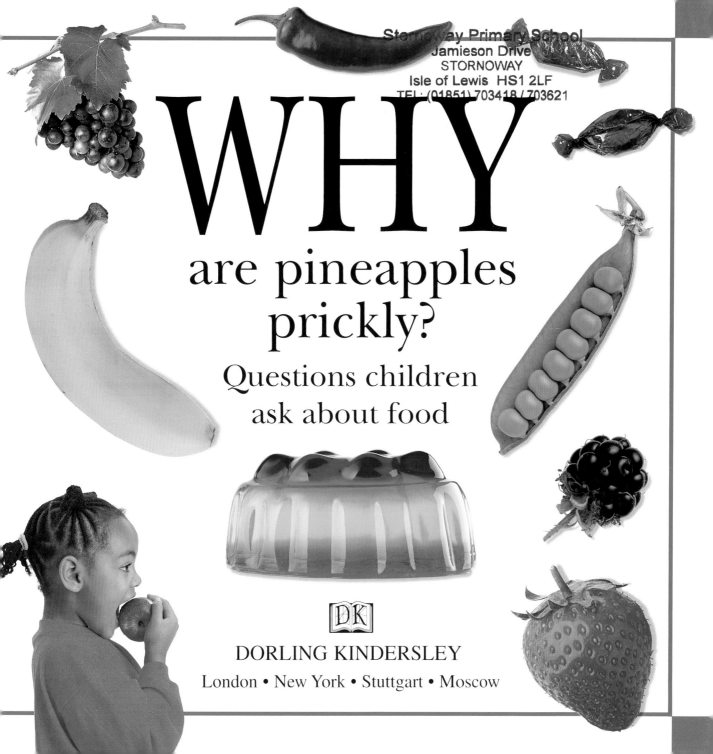

DK

DORLING KINDERSLEY

London • New York • Stuttgart • Moscow

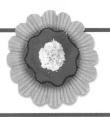

Why do jellies

Jelly is made from fruit juice, gelatin and hot water. They bond together and form a solid as the water cools. But the bonds are weak, so the jelly wobbles.

Why does ice cream melt?
Ice cream is a mixture of eggs, sugar, cream and flavourings

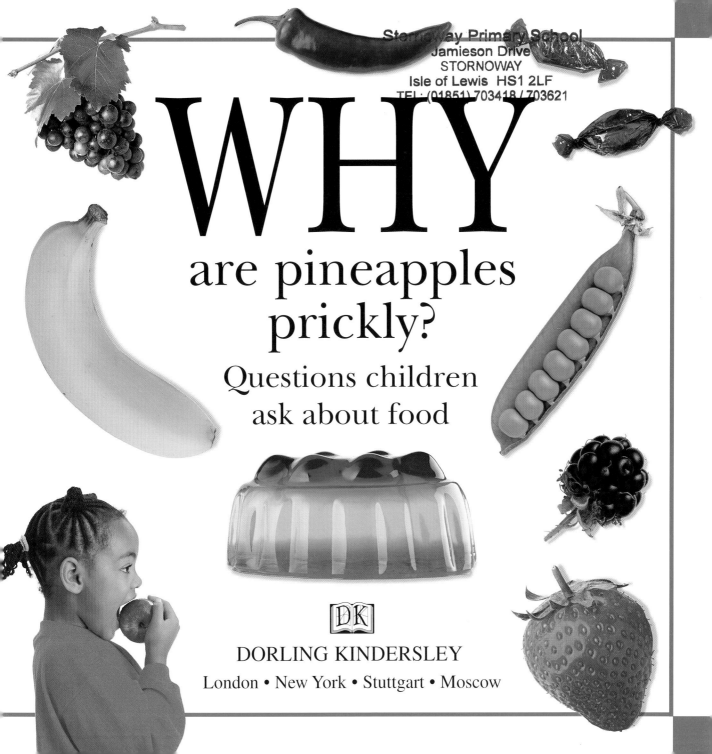

WHY
are pineapples prickly?

Questions children
ask about food

DK

DORLING KINDERSLEY
London • New York • Stuttgart • Moscow

Why do jellies

Jelly is made from fruit juice, gelatin and hot water. They bond together and form a solid as the water cools. But the bonds are weak, so the jelly wobbles.

Why does ice cream melt?
Ice cream is a mixture of eggs, sugar, cream and flavourings

wobble?

Why are there bubbles in my drink?
Bubbles of carbon dioxide can be forced into a drink at the factory to make it fizzy. When you open the drink, the bubbles start to escape.

that is frozen into its solid state. Just like snow, if it is exposed to heat, it will turn back to liquid.

Why do some things

Sweet food contains lots of sugar. When it touches taste-buds on your tongue, messages are sent to your brain about its sweet flavour.

Why are chillies hot?
They're not hot to touch, but if you bite one the chemicals inside irritate and burn your mouth.

taste sweet?

Why are lemons sour?
Citrus fruits such as lemons, limes, grapefruit and oranges, all contain a small amount of citric acid in their juices. Citric acid tastes sour.

Why do crisps make me thirsty?
Salt absorbs water. If you eat salty crisps, your mouth tells your brain that you need a drink.

Why does rice grow

Rice is a type of grass that needs warm weather and lots of water to grow. Rice is planted in flooded fields to give the plants all the moisture they need to produce rice grains. The fields are drained before the rice is harvested.

Why do some peas hide in pods?
Peas are pea plant seeds, and grow in pods like beans. We eat most seeds and

underwater?

Why is tea brown?
Tea is made by soaking tea leaves in hot water. The leaves contain chemicals called tannins, which dissolve in the water. Tannins are used to make dyes – in this case they dye the water brown.

pods together, but pea pods can be too thick and tough, so we take the peas out.

Why do apples

Cores contain pips, the seeds of the apple tree. The apples are eaten by animals and birds, who then scatter pips in their droppings.

Why are potatoes dirty?
Potatoes are swollen parts of the plant's stems

have cores?

Why do peaches have stones inside?
A stone is the tough case that protects a peach seed from greedy insects. If a stone is planted, the seed inside may sprout and start to grow.

that form underground to store nutrients. These swellings are called tubers. We dig them up, wash, then cook them.

Why is fruit good

Fruit is rich in the vitamins and minerals we need to keep us healthy.

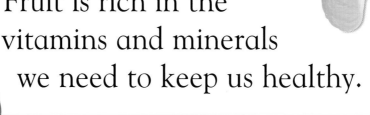

Why does fruit change colour?
As the seeds inside a fruit mature, chemicals in the fruit change its colour. The bright colours attract animals and let them know that the fruit is sweet and ready to eat.

for me?

Fruit also contains plenty of fibre which helps our digestion.

Why do we wash fruit and vegetables?
Fruit and vegetables are sprayed with chemicals to keep away insects. We wash off these chemicals, and we also peel skin that is too tough to eat.

Why are pineapples

Pineapple plants have very sharp, spiny leaves that grow all around and on top of the pineapple to protect the fruit from hungry animals as it grows.

Why do farmers flood cranberry fields?
The fields are flooded in order

prickly?

Why are raisins wrinkly?
Raisins are actually dried grapes. As they lose water, they shrivel up and shrink and their skin turns wrinkly and brown.

Why are coconuts so rough?
The hard shell and rough, hairy layer of a coconut help to keep the milk and flesh inside from drying out.

to harvest the berries. They are shaken loose, then float to the surface to be gathered.

Why do some people

Grown-ups eat more than children because their bigger bodies need more energy. Some people, like athletes, need to eat lots of food as they use up a huge amount of energy when they train and race.

Why do onions make me cry?
When we slice an onion it gives off strong chemicals that sting

eat more than others?

Why are carrots good for our eyes?
Carrots, like other fresh vegetables, contain vitamin A. We need vitamin A to keep our skin and hair healthy, as well as our eyes.

our eyes. Our eyes run with tears to wash out the chemicals.

Why don't the eggs

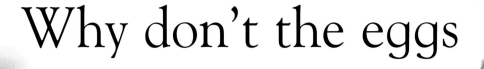

Eggs from shops never have chicks inside them because they have not been fertilised by

Why is it called a hamburger if it's not made from ham?
The hamburger is actually named after Hamburg, a city in Germany, where it was first invented.

we eat have chicks inside?

a cockerel. A fertilised egg must be kept warm so that the chick inside can grow and hatch.

Why don't fruit trees grow inside me? You might accidentally swallow a fruit seed, but it will pass straight through your body, or your digestive juices will break it down.